HOW TO DEAL

UNDERSTANDING FRIENDSHIP

MARIE-THERESE MILLER, Ph.D.

Rourke Educational Media | A Division of Carson Dellosa Education

rourkeeducationalmedia.com

ROURKE'S
SCHOOL to HOME
CONNECTIONS
BEFORE AND DURING READING ACTIVITIES

Before Reading: *Building Background Knowledge and Vocabulary*

Building background knowledge can help children process new information and build upon what they already know. Before reading a book, it is important to tap into what children already know about the topic. This will help them develop their vocabulary and increase their reading comprehension.

Questions and Activities to Build Background Knowledge:

1. Look at the front cover of the book and read the title. What do you think this book will be about?
2. What do you already know about this topic?
3. Take a book walk and skim the pages. Look at the table of contents, photographs, captions, and bold words. Did these text features give you any information or predictions about what you will read in this book?

Vocabulary: *Vocabulary Is Key to Reading Comprehension*

Use the following directions to prompt a conversation about each word.

- Read the vocabulary words.
- What comes to mind when you see each word?
- What do you think each word means?

Vocabulary Words:

- *abundance*
- *critical*
- *enriching*
- *grieve*
- *interrogating*
- *isolating*
- *overwhelm*
- *parallel*
- *reliable*
- *reputation*
- *sincere*
- *superior*

During Reading: *Reading for Meaning and Understanding*

To achieve deep comprehension of a book, children are encouraged to use close reading strategies. During reading, it is important to have children stop and make connections. These connections result in deeper analysis and understanding of a book.

Close Reading a Text

During reading, have children stop and talk about the following:

- Any confusing parts
- Any unknown words
- Text to text, text to self, text to world connections
- The main idea in each chapter or heading

Encourage children to use context clues to determine the meaning of any unknown words. These strategies will help children learn to analyze the text more thoroughly as they read.

When you are finished reading this book, turn to page 46 for **Text-Dependent Questions** and an **Extension Activity**.

TABLE OF CONTENTS

CHAPTER 1

HOW TO MEET FRIENDS

One chilly morning at the bus stop, Jess thought, *I hate being new in the neighborhood. I wish I had a friend to sit with on the school bus.* Just then, a helicopter whirred overhead. Jess turned to the girl beside her and said, "That helicopter is low enough to land on the roof of my house."

The girl, Meghan, said, "The helicopter is keeping warm air flowing over our apple trees so they don't freeze. We own the apple orchard across the street."

"Cool," Jess said. "Apples are my favorite." Jess and Meghan sat next to each other and talked about apple cider, pies, and other foods they liked all the way to school.

Friendships are an important and **enriching** part of life. With friends, you can share thoughts and feelings—and fun. Your friends help you appreciate the similarities and differences we have as human beings. But where and how can you make that friendship connection?

School is a great place to make friends: in the classroom, at lunch, or during gym class. You can follow your interests and join an after-school club or sports team. The people you meet at these activities might share your passions, which is a solid start to friendship.

Your community also offers many chances for meeting friends. You could volunteer to teach crafts at the library story hour, for example. The people you meet while volunteering may share your values and make great friends.

Consider your neighbors, just as Jess and Meghan did. When you befriend someone who lives three houses away, you have a person who is close by for daily bike rides and kickball games—no parental transportation needed. Your own family members, cousins and siblings, can also become your close friends.

First Approach

School psychologist Jennifer Obrizok recommends talking to new people one-on-one. It is less nerve-racking than going up to a group to begin a conversation. So join that person sitting alone in the cafeteria and start chatting.

Your Body Speaks

When you meet a potential friend, make sure your body language is welcoming and friendly. Stand up straight, uncross your arms, make eye contact, and smile!

Now, what to say to break the ice? You could talk about your shared experiences, as Jess did with her comments about the helicopter. You could ask for a bit of help: "Can you show me how to do that jump shot?" You might use your powers of observation and ask a question. For example, if a girl has a cello strapped to her back, you could ask, "What is your favorite piece of music to perform?" Finally, you might offer a **sincere** compliment: "Those are great boots! Where did you find them?" By the way, remember to introduce yourself after you break the ice.

No Whining

Think about how you feel when someone you are talking to is complaining about something. It's not pleasant, is it? It's not a good idea to start a first conversation with a complaint. Complaining suggests that you see the world negatively, which probably will not attract the upbeat friend that you seek. Humor, however, is a terrific conversation starter.

CHAPTER 2

THE GOOD FRIEND

“I’m playing the saxophone in the school talent show next Saturday,” Jack told his close friend, Hameed.

“I’ll be there,” Hameed promised him.

But two days later, another friend of Hameed’s offered him a ticket to scc his favorite professional baseball team play. The game was on the same night as the talent show. Hameed could imagine the taste of the hot dogs and the crack of the bat hitting the ball. He really wanted to go to that game.

At the talent show, the host announced, “First prize goes to Jack.” Hameed jumped to his feet and cheered louder than anyone else in the auditorium. He was so proud of his friend!

A good friend makes your life better. After you spend time with a close friend, you feel good about yourself and what you did together.

Good friends act in certain ways. First of all, a close friend shows up in person to share experiences, as Hameed did for Jack. There is no replacement for what teacher Donna Desimone calls "real-life face time."

Friends are also **reliable**. If you make plans, follow through with them—even if something that seems more exciting comes along, like Hameed's baseball game.

Be Flexible

You won't share all the same interests as your friends. But don't limit yourself to your own interests. Maybe your friend is obsessed with King Arthur and suggests a visit to the medieval fair. Sir Gawain and his buddies might not call to you, but give it a try. The fun is found in the time you spend together.

Friends give one another emotional support. A friend encourages your goals and celebrates your successes. Hameed was this kind of cheerleader for Jack. There is no room for jealousy in friendship. Try not to think: *It's not fair. Elizabeth landed the lead in the musical.* Consider the idea of **abundance**, which means there are enough good opportunities to go around. Anyway, everyone has their own special talents and strengths, so there is no need to compare.

Finally, good friendships are balanced. They are reciprocal. For instance, one friend shouldn't always be the one texting the other or making all the plans.

Rough Moments

If your friend is going through a tough time, practice empathy by imagining how they feel. If your friend's poodle dies, listen to them express sadness and offer a hug. You might even perform a small act of kindness and frame a photo of your friend and their furry companion as a gift.

CHAPTER 3

FRIENDSHIP TROUBLES

Allie looked her friend Marta up and down. "A shirt with a sequined owl? Really? It's so childish," Allie said.

Marta frowned. "Well, I like owls."

"You should choose something more fashionable now that we're in middle school," Allie told her.

"Anyway," Marta said, changing the subject, "I'm super excited about my soccer tryouts tomorrow. I think I have a chance at a good position."

"Calm down," Allie said. "Lots of girls are better players than you."

Marta felt like a deflated balloon.

Even the closest friends experience some difficulties. You have to consider if the problem can be fixed or if it is time to move away from your friendship.

A common problem in friendship is gossip, or telling others a friend's secrets and private business. Friends need to be able to trust one another, so you need to keep their secrets to yourself. If you spill private information, you will gain a **reputation** as a blabbermouth. Then, no friends will share their innermost thoughts with you.

Secrets to Share

There are times when you should not keep a secret, advises social worker Nancy Kelly. If a secret is harming your friend—for example, if they are abusing drugs or have stopped eating—you should always tell a trusted adult. In this way, you are being a good friend because you are getting your friend help and keeping them safe.

A friend who is too **critical**, like Allie was with Marta, is a problem. The criticism made Marta feel bad about herself and her abilities. Good friends build you up, they don't tear you down. A friend who is too competitive, who says, "I get more As" or "I score more goals than you do," can hurt the way you value yourself.

Gossips

Some people don't gossip at all. Some gossip all the time! There are reasons people gossip about others, and none are a good excuse for this behavior. A gossip might be jealous or trying to make themselves feel ***superior****. Sometimes, they want to add excitement to their lives—at the expense of another person.*

Do you have a friend who is constantly complaining? This negative view of things can be draining for friends.

Finally, beware the one-sided friendship. A friend who asks you to buy them a snack every day, but never buys one for you, is likely using you. A friend who takes advantage of you is not a true friend.

When friendship difficulties crop up, you can try to work it out by talking to your friend. Or, you might decide to end the friendship. You could make yourself unavailable to the friend quietly or you might say directly, “I think we should take a break and find other friends.” A trusted adult can provide tips for untying a friendship gracefully.

Be True to You

Author Pascale Perrier says that your values should ***parallel*** *the values of your friends. She says to ask yourself: Do I agree with their way of looking at things? If they tease others, for instance, distance yourself and find new friends. Certainly, if they do dangerous things, run the other way.*

CHAPTER

4

TALKING IT OUT

Greyson attached a leash to the collar of a Chihuahua. He joined Sebastian, who was walking a Boxer mix in the woods across from the animal shelter where they both volunteered.

"I have a Rhodesian Ridgeback and a ferret at home," Sebastian told Greyson.

"Wow! I wish I had a dog," Greyson said. "But I'm glad I get to play with them here."

"I hope you get one soon," Sebastian said. "Did you know that Rhodesian Ridgebacks were originally from Africa and they were used to hunt lions?"

"That's so cool! Is your dog strong and fast?" Greyson asked.

Sebastian nodded. "She is. You should come to my house and meet her."

Communication is the way to keep a friendship going and growing. Conversation is a back and forth—like a tennis game. Notice the way Greyson and Sebastian kept hitting the conversation ball over the net.

You can ask questions to keep the conversation alive. People enjoy talking about themselves. But don't act like a police officer **interrogating** a suspect.

Be an active listener. Don't glance at your phone. You could follow up with comments that showed you were paying attention.

When it's your turn to talk, reveal a bit about yourself. This is how friends learn about one another. Do this gradually, though. Over-sharing private information can **overwhelm** a friend. And try not to make it all about you. Sebastian did not give a 20-minute speech about how he trained his ferret to use a litter box.

Communication is key when trying to solve a problem with a friend. Let's say that your friend isn't eating lunch with you and you are angry about it. Meet them in a quiet, private place. Start with a positive comment, such as, "We've been close friends for a long time." Then, use statements that begin with "I" such as, "I miss laughing with you at lunch." Using "you" statements, such as, "You keep ditching me" will put your friend on the defensive.

Listen to your friend's response and try to understand their point of view. Maybe they have a good explanation, such as the need to work with other students on a group project. Finally, have a clear solution in mind. For example, say, "Let's plan to eat together at least twice a week."

Forgiveness

Have you done something to hurt your friend? Say you are sorry as soon as possible and make the apology sincere. If your friend apologizes to you, forgive them. We all make mistakes.

CHAPTER 5

TECH AND FRIENDSHIP

Anisha texted Xander, "Do you want to come over and watch a scary movie tonight?"

"Sounds good," Xander wrote back.

Anisha popped some popcorn and chose a few movie possibilities. But Xander didn't come.

Anisha was angry. "I can't believe you didn't show up," she textcd. "You are a terrible friend."

"So sorry," Xander replied.

Anisha didn't think Xander really sounded sorry. This made her angrier. She ignored him the next day at school when he tried to explain. When she finally talked to him, he told her there had been an emergency with his little sister. Anisha felt terrible for the way she treated her friend.

Technology has its positive and negative sides where friendship is concerned. Technology and social media make it possible to keep in touch with friends when you can't be together in person. This is especially great when a close friend has moved far away.

In addition, you can easily use technology to make plans to meet up with friends in real life. Many times, you can even find fun and interesting local events posted on social media that you and your friends can attend.

On the other hand, technology can be **isolating**. If you are constantly on your phone or computer, you will miss out on real-life friends and activities.

Using technology to communicate can also cause problems. People are more likely to write hurtful or angry things when they aren't face-to-face. Anisha probably would not have used such angry words if Xander were standing in front of her.

Also, conversation via text or social media can be misunderstood because you can't see the person's facial expressions or hear their tone of voice. Anisha might have realized that Xander's "So sorry" was sincere if she had seen the tears in his eyes or heard the sadness in his voice. But in the text, it doesn't seem like he is truly sorry.

Just Walk Away

Social worker Kathleen Murphy has this advice: If you feel angry or hurt, walk away from technology before you write anything. Let your emotions flow through you, and they will become less strong. Then, you can respond to your friend instead of reacting. Consider responding in person, which is often the better way.

Super Sad? There's Help

Sometimes, you might feel alone and think that everyone is against you. You might experience low moods, which can lead to thoughts of self-harm or suicide. Always tell someone such as a parent, relative, teacher, clergy member, or medical professional who can help you get the support you need. The National Suicide Prevention Lifeline is available 24 hours a day to provide help at 1-800-273-8255.

CHAPTER 6

BE YOUR OWN BEST FRIEND

Grace and Dawn started sleeping over at each other's homes in kindergarten. They played board games, made funny videos, and baked snacks. The two were the best of friends all through elementary school.

But things changed when they got to middle school. Dawn joined the cross-country team. She spent most of her time with her teammates.

Grace still called Dawn often. "Dawn, do you want to sleep over, play cards, and bake brownies?"

"I have to clean my room," Dawn often replied.

Each time Grace called, Dawn had another excuse for not getting together. It became clear that Dawn had new interests and new friends. She didn't want to be Grace's friend anymore.

Grace was heartbroken.

Friendship is great, but it is also good to enjoy moments alone. Being alone does not have to mean feeling lonely. Take time to be on your own and get to know who you are and what you want in life. "You have to be happy with yourself. Be your own best friend," Jennifer Obrizok says. "Treat yourself well, you deserve it."

In Grace's case, she can use some time by herself to **grieve** the loss of her friendship with Dawn. She can be kind to herself, do exactly what she thinks is fun to do, and heal.

She could read that book from the library she has been eyeing. She can relax in hot baths. She might binge-watch her favorite show. Finally, she can make plans for meeting new friends and imagine the exciting adventures they will have together.

Friends share life's happy and challenging times. They talk, laugh, and create memories together. Knowing how to be an understanding, reliable friend helps you establish meaningful friendships with others who share the same positive qualities.

Ditch Labels

Author Dr. Laurie Zelinger advises, "Let go of labels." Don't let terms such as "jock" or "nerd" limit the way you see yourself or others. People are more complex than labels. If you look beyond labels, you might find friends.

ACTIVITY

FRIENDSHIP TICKETS

Make your friend a book of tickets for adventures you can share. Cut poster board into small rectangles for tickets. Leave the left edge of each ticket blank. On the remaining portion, write the name of a fun activity such as *Bake Cookies* or *Watch a Movie*. Decorate the tickets with markers, colored pencils, or other supplies. Create as many tickets as you wish to honor.

Stack the tickets together. Punch two holes at the left side of each ticket. Then, thread both ends of a length of ribbon up through the holes. Tie a bow to bind the tickets into a booklet.

Give the tickets to a friend for a birthday, a holiday, or as an everyday act of kindness. It is a present you will both enjoy!

GLOSSARY

abundance (uh-BUHN-duhns): a great quantity

critical (KRIT-i-kuhl): inclined to express a negative opinion or to find fault

enriching (en-RICH-ing): improving something by adding good things to it

grieve (greev): to feel intense sorrow, usually because someone you love has died or gone away

interrogating (in-TAIR-uh-gate-ing): questioning someone in detail, usually in connection with a crime

isolating (EYE-suh-late-ing): keeping something or someone alone or separate

overwhelm (oh-vur-WELM): to have a very strong emotional effect

parallel (PAR-uh-lel): to match

reliable (ri-LYE-uh-buhl): able to be depended upon or trusted

reputation (rep-yuh-TAY-shuhn): your worth or character, as judged by other people

sincere (sin-SEER): straightforward and honest

superior (su-PEER-ee-ur): believing or behaving as if you are better than other people

INDEX

TEXT-DEPENDENT QUESTIONS

1. What are some good places to meet friends?
2. How can you start a conversation with someone you just met?
3. How does a good friend behave?
4. What is gossip and why do people gossip?
5. Why are texts sometimes misunderstood?

EXTENSION ACTIVITY

Write a short fictional story about close friends. Consider what behaviors and qualities make a good friend. What do the friends do together? What adventures do they have? How do they treat one another? Include a conflict between the friends and have them solve it with healthy communication.

BIBLIOGRAPHY

Cain, Susan, Gregory Mone, and Erica Mroz. *Quiet Power: The Secret Strengths of Introverts.* New York: Dial Books for Young Readers, 2016.

Criswell, Patti Kelley. *A Smart Girl's Guide to Friendship Troubles: Dealing with Fights, Being Left Out, and the Whole Popularity Thing.* Middleton, Wisconsin: American Girl Publishing, 2003.

Criswell, Patti Kelley. *Friends: Making Them and Keeping Them.* Middleton, Wisconsin: American Girl Publishing, 2006.

Desimone, Donna, TOH. (Program Instructor, Community Steps to Independence. Cresskill, New Jersey), Interview with the author. 27 October 2018.

Gabor, Don. *How to Start a Conversation and Make Friends.* Clinton, Massachusetts: Legacy Publishing Group, 1983.

Hemmen, Lucie, Ph.D. *The Teen Girl's Survival Guide: 10 Tips for Making Friends, Avoiding Drama & Coping with Social Stress.* Oakland, California: Instant Help Books, 2015.

Holyoke, Nancy. *A Smart Girl's Guide: Drama, Rumors, and Secrets.* Middleton, Wisconsin: American Girl Publishing, 2015.

Kelly, Nancy, LCSW-R. (Clinical Unit Administrator–Forensics, Dutchess County Department of Community and Behavioral Health, Poughkeepsie, New York), Interview with the author. 22 October 2018.

Murphy, Kathleen, MSW, LSW. (Mindfulness Meditation Specialist, Bluffton, South Carolina), Interview with the author. 19 October 2018.

Obrizok, Jennifer. (School Psychologist, Millbrook Middle School, Millbrook, New York), Interview with the author. 12 October 2018.

Perrier, Pascale. *Flying Solo: How to Soar Above Your Lonely Feelings, Make Friends, and Find the Happiest You.* New York: Harry N. Abrams, 2007.

Roberts, Emily, MA, LPC. *Express Yourself: A Teen Girl's Guide to Speaking Up and Being Who You Are.* Oakland, California: Instant Help Books, 2015.

Zelinger, Laurie, Ph.D. *A Smart Girl's Guide to Liking Herself–Even on the Bad Days.* Middleton, Wisconsin: American Girl Publishing. 2012.

ABOUT THE AUTHOR

Marie-Therese Miller is the author of *The Dog Tales* series about working dogs, *Managing Responsibilities*, and *Rachel Carson*. She holds a Ph.D. from St. John's University, where her scholarly focus was James Thurber and humor. Miller and her husband, John, have five children.

www.rourkeeducationalmedia.com

PHOTO CREDITS: Cover: Top photo © VGstockstudio | Shutterstock.com, Bottom photo © Syda Productions | Shutterstock.com; Title page © VGstockstudio | Shutterstock.com,Page 4-5: istock.com | LightFieldStudios, Page 6-7: Shutterstock.com | By SeventyFour, istock.com | KatarzynaBialasiewicz, istock.com | Rawpixel. Page 8-9: istock.com | LightFieldStudios, istock.com | Михаил Руденко.Page 10-11: istock.com | monkeybusinessimages, shutterstock.com | Anatoliy Karlyuk. Page 12-13: istock.com | jamirae. Page 14-15: istock.com | Wavebreakmedia. istock.com | Wavebreakmedia. Page 16-17: shutterstock.com | Yerchak Uladzimir, shutterstock.com | MPH Photos, istock.com | diego_cervo. Page 18-19: shutterstock.com | ekmelica, istock.com | Wavebreakmedia. shutterstock.com | Dean Clarke Page 20-21: istock.com | Daisy-Daisy, 138342872 ©Mikhail Azarov | Dreamstime.com, istock.com | monkeybusinessimages. Page 22-23: istock.com | Daisy-Daisy, 79850064 ©Iakov Filimonov | Dreamstime.com, stock.com | Antonio_Diaz. Page 24-25: istock.com | fizkes, istock.com | 1BSG, istock.com | 1BSG. Page 26-27: istock.com | pyotr021, shutterstock.com | eurobanks, 136092599 ©Vasilis Ververidis | Dreamstime.com. Page 28-29: istock.com | Highwaystarz-Photography, 92907366 ©Nataliia Prokofyeva | Dreamstime.com. Page 30-31: istock.com | Highwaystarz-Photography, istock.com | Highwaystarz-Photography, istock.com | JackF. Page 32-33: istock.com | doble-d, istock.com | jacoblund. Page 34-35: istock.com | Antonio_Diaz, istock.com | bigtunaonline, istock.com | ntonio_Diaz. Page 36-37: istock.com | monkeybusinessimages, istock.com | jacoblund, istock.com | AntonioGuillem. Page 38-39: istock.com | BVDC, istock.com | KatarzynaBialasiewicz. Page 40-41: istock.com | BravissimoS, istock.com | KatarzynaBialasiewicz. Page 42-43: istock.com | patat, istock.com | jacoblund.

Edited by: Kim Thompson

Produced by Blue Door Education for Rourke Educational Media. Cover and interior design by: Jennifer Dydyk

Library of Congress PCN Data

Understanding Friendship / Marie-Therese Miller, Ph.D.
(How to Deal)
ISBN 978-1-73161-487-2 (hard cover)
ISBN 978-1-73161-294-6 (soft cover)
ISBN 978-1-73161-592-3 (e-Book)
ISBN 978-1-73161-697-5 (e-Pub)
Library of Congress Control Number: 2019932381

Rourke Educational Media
Printed in the United States of America,
North Mankato, Minnesota